Warning

IMPROPER USE OF THE CONTENTS DESCRIBED HEREIN MAY RESULT IN SERIOUS INJURY. THE ACTIVITIES SHOULD NOT BE ATTEMPTED WITHOUT THE SUPERVISION OF TRAINED AND PROPERLY QUALIFIED LEADERS.

NEITHER THE AUTHOR, NOR THE PUBLISHER, NOR THE SELLER, NOR ANY DISTRIBUTOR OF THIS PUBLICATION ASSUMES ANY LIABILITY FOR LOSS OR DAMAGE, DIRECT OR CONSEQUENTIAL TO THE READER OR OTHERS RESULTING FROM THE USE OF THE MATERIALS CONTAINED HEREIN, WHETHER SUCH LOSS OR DAMAGE RESULTS FROM ERRORS, OMISSIONS, AMBIGUITIES, OR INACCURACIES IN THE MATERIALS CONTAINED HEREIN OR OTHERWISE. NO WARRANTIES, EXPRESS OR IMPLIED, AS TO MERCHANTABILITY OR AS TO FITNESS FOR ANY PARTICULAR USE OR PURPOSE ARE INTENDED TO ARISE OUT OF THE SALE OR DISTRIBUTION OF THIS PUBLICATION, AND THIS PUBLICATION IS SOLD "AS IS" AND "WITH ALL FAULTS." THE LIABILITY OF THE AUTHOR, PUBLISHER, SELLER, OR ANY DISTRIBUTOR OF THIS PUBLICATION ON ACCOUNT OF ANY SUCH ERRORS, OMISSIONS, OR AMBIGUITIES, SHALL IN ANY EVENT, BE LIMITED TO THE PURCHASE PRICE OF THIS PUBLICATION.

Preface

Thank you very much for choosing *Catchin' the Carrot*. I know you will find this easy to use personal planning tool beneficial in scripting a strategic direction for your prosperity. I look forward to hearing your stories of success.

If you have any questions along the way about how to use this tool, please don't hesitate to contact our offices online at *www.tylerhayden.com* and we will get back to you promptly.

Again, thank you for choosing *Catchin' the Carrot*. I look forward to hearing of your personal prosperity.

Tyler Hayden

For more personal development tools or to book a live presentation, contact your favorite speaker's bureau or visit us online at:

www.tylerhayden.com

After my speaking engagements, without fail someone asks me, "What 'things' did you do to achieve such great prosperity at such a young age?" Frankly, I feel embarrassed by that question. I'm a pretty plain and simple guy. I pump my own gas. I love my family. I even take out my own trash and recyclables. So I didn't know what these "things" were that people were asking me about.

It has taken me a long time to realize that even though I'm no different than anyone else, I guess I approach life differently. That is what *Catchin' the Carrot* is all about, achieving "things" – differently.

What do I mean by differently? Well, differently is made up of a few "things" that all lead to one magnificent "thing." Those few "things" are individual life components that all affect the magnificent "thing," which is you.

What I did differently from a lot of people I know is I got to know myself first and then I built a life around me that made me happy. Most of my friends and colleagues did it the other way around, trying to make themselves happy by surrounding themselves with the life components that should make a person happy. Eventually, they settle into a place where they are happy or learn to be happy in the place they end up.

My friends, never settle. Take the initially more difficult road of knowing yourself first and then build a life around you that will energize you. That is the "thing" that matters.

I'm going to help you do this "thing" with *Catchin' the Carrot*, by taking you through eight easy steps. That is the beginning. After we have completed this process, you will need to refer to your work every month or so and adjust its content accordingly because you are going to start changing your life before your very eyes. Although this is a lifelong process, the sooner you start investing time in getting to know yourself, the sooner you will realize the benefits.

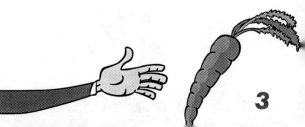

Write a brief introduction about yourself. It's your ten-second personal selling pitch. What you are going to write is what you would say to the "CEO of Life" if you had ten seconds to sell the fact that you are the right person for the job. Your statement should detail:

- the most important "things" in your life;
- your personal history;
- where you see yourself in the future.

Give it a shot right now. Make a mental note to come back to this and adjust it once you have completed the plan. You will learn things about yourself as you go, and this statement will need to be revised.

Every great corporation has a mission statement that drives the organization to success. For *Catchin' the Carrot* you need to know what yours is so you, too, will be driven to success.

Your mission needs to be a short rallying cry that you can easily remember. For example, "Jenny Cardouchi is an outgoing, trustworthy person who achieves high performance reviews at work and is an active community volunteer," or, "Jack MacDonald is a quiet, athletic person who excels at repairing foreign and domestic automobiles while finding quality time to spend with his family and friends."

Your statement should answer the following questions:

- What function will you perform as an individual?
- For whom do you perform this function?
- How do you go about performing this function?

What?

Whom?

How?

Mission...

Values

I n every decision we make as individuals there is a set of values that influence that decision. You might choose not to litter because you value the environment that we live in, or you might practice layups because you value your basketball team's success. What we do can often be explained by our core values.

What are your core values? Family? Friends? Success? Health? Money? Learning? Respect? The possibilities are as diverse as we are. Some of my core values are respect for others, being a cutting-edge educator, having fun, caring for the ones I love, and maintaining the highest standards in everything I do. Understanding your values will help you to better understand yourself and execute better decisions.

What are your values? List them below and then choose a maximum of three.

_____   _____

_____   _____

_____   _____

_____   _____

_____   _____

Top 3
Values...

_____   _____

_____   _____

_____   _____   ┌─────────────┐
                                     │   │
                                     │   │
                                     └─────────────┘
_____   _____

_____   _____

_____   _____   ┌─────────────┐
                                     │   │
                                     │   │
                                     └─────────────┘
_____   _____

_____   _____

_____   _____   ┌─────────────┐
                                     │   │
                                     │   │
                                     └─────────────┘
_____   _____

_____   _____

_____   _____

Objectives

Take a moment to reread your personal mission. What have you committed to achieve in that statement? What are the things that you need to do to achieve it? Do you need to, for example, take night courses, begin volunteering for company projects, or spend more time with your family? What specific steps do you need to take to achieve that mission?

In the following section, set objectives that will help you to achieve your mission. Your objectives should be S.M.A.R.T. (Simple, Measurable, Achievable, Realistic, and Time Dependent). For example, one of Jack's might be to open a foreign car repair business in 2010, or take his family on annual week-long summer vacations starting this summer. What specific things do you need to do to achieve your objectives?

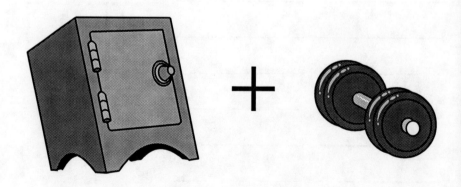

Objective 1

_____

_____

_____

Objective 2

_____

_____

_____

Objective 3

_____

_____

_____

Objective 4

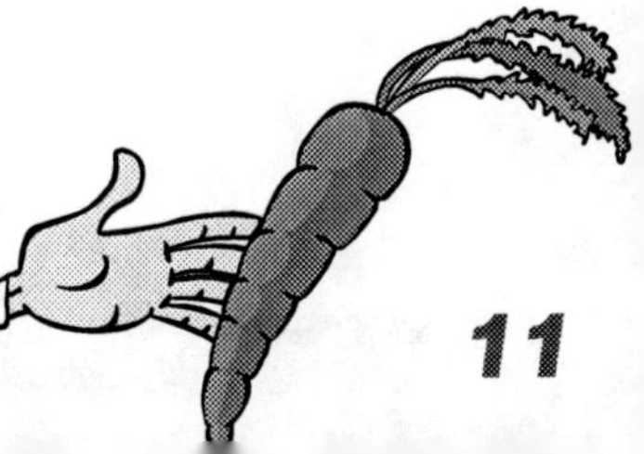

_____

_____

_____

I n *Catchin' the Carrot* it is important that you make proactive decisions, not reactive ones. Reactive means when something happens you take action towards it. For example, if the phone rings you answer it. Proactive refers to when you plan how to respond before something happens. For example, knowing how to escape from your home in the event of a fire before it happens. By completing the following, you will be proactively planning what could affect you on your path to prosperity.

Think about the things that affect the way you live. Consider some of the macro influences, such as social relationships (i.e., family, significant others, etc.), political factors (i.e., government, laws, taxes, etc.), technological developments (i.e., computers, transportation, etc.), and economic considerations (i.e., loans, job, etc.). Think in terms of these macro influences and how they affect your mission and then write them down.

Now, evaluate to what extent these things will affect your mission, ranking them as severe, moderate, or slight. For example, for Jenny's mission, an economic impact might be, "currently able to save only enough money for one class a year," which I would evaluate as a moderate impact. Do this for all the things you identified in your environmental scan.

Environmental Scan	Rank

You and I each have our own personal and professional strengths and weaknesses. You might be a skilled reader (strength) but weak at doing math (weakness). I might be great at motivating people (strength) but weak at meeting deadlines (weakness). Also, you and I are surrounded by personal and professional opportunities and threats. You might live close to a large potential client base (opportunity) but have six major competitors in the same industrial park (threat). I might have great genes for a healthy body (opportunity) but not know the proper techniques for exercising (threat).

By understanding these factors, we can maximize those things that benefit us and manage those that could hold us back. So take a serious look at how you are using your strengths and weaknesses in your life. What changes could you make in your favor?

In the following squares, brainstorm your personal and professional strengths and weaknesses, opportunities and threats.

Strengths

Weaknesses

Opportunities

Threats

Action Planning

Think of your mission as the top of a staircase, your objectives are the stairs, and action planning is each movement that you must make in order to physically step onto a stair.

Action planning is about writing down what you need to do specifically to achieve your objectives. Start by writing down the objectives that you identified earlier in this process. Then focus on each objective individually and write down the movements (or actions) that you must make in order to achieve that objective. For example, one of Jack's objectives was to "take an annual week-long summer vacation with family starting this summer." His action steps might be to:

1. start saving $150/month in a special savings account;
2. sit down with the family to discuss what they would like to do that summer;
3. research options for a week-long vacation;
4. make necessary travel arrangements (flight, hotels, vacation time, etc.).

You get the idea. Now try it for yourself.

Objective 1

_____

_____

_____

Objective 2

_____

_____

_____

Objective 3

_____

_____

_____

Objective 4

_____

_____

_____

Five-Year Strategy

In the previous stage you completed an action plan for *Catchin' the Carrot*. In doing so, you have decided what the steps are that will help you climb the stairs towards your mission. Now you need to take all those action steps and sequence them in manageable blocks that will enable you to achieve them in a logical order.

Write the dates for the next five years (i.e., 2004, 2005, 2006, etc.). Under each date write in point form the action steps that you will complete prior to that year's end. For example, in Jenny's plan for the year 2004 she will:

- apply for a Business Administration Degree at *Acadia University*;
- explore gaps in human resource provision at her current place of employment as a personal project;
- meet with her manager to express an interest in volunteering on company committees;
- create and commit to an aerobic training program three days a week;
- spend time camping at least one weekend a month.

Once you have done this final step, start putting your plan in motion. Start living your mission, expressing your values, working on your action steps, identifying your opportunities, and *Catchin' the Carrot*.

Year 1

Year 2

Year 3

Year 4

Year 5

Invite Tyler to Perform a Powerful Keynote Presentation

Laugh uncontrollably and learn unknowingly with Tyler's 100 percent satisfaction guaranteed presentations.
If you are looking for a stuffed shirt and a quick nap, Tyler's definitely not your man. His shows are innovative, fast paced, and interactive – we don't mean just flashy PowerPoint. We mean flying rubber chickens, new sports cars, and exploding rubber gloves! So please make sure that your chair backs are up, your tray tables are in an upright position, and your seatbelts are fastened, because Tyler Hayden's shows are one heck of a ride!

Livin' Life Large
Discover how to get the most out of every single moment of every single day with Tyler's prescription for Livin' Life Large.

Catchin' the Carrot
Using Tyler's powerful personal strategic planning tool, you can actually Catch the Carrot you have been chasing for a long time.

The Greatest Gifts
Learn to lead authentically by rewarding yourself and others continually with the Greatest Gifts.

Friday!
Approach every day like it's Friday – by living, laughing, and learning.

Customized Keynote Presentation

Meeting his clients' specific desired presentation outcomes is Tyler's specialty. Invite him to tailor a presentation just for you.

Give us a call toll free at 866.4.GO.PLAY (866.446.7529) or check us out online at www.tylerhayden.com and inquire about having Tyler work with your conference, convention, meeting, or retreat! I'm sure you will agree that he's like mainlining caffeine. (Just check out his video online.)

Team-building Adventures for your Group

Our trainers will bring our adventures to your place of work. Through a series of nontraditional team-building events, we will transform your group into an effective team. Their energy will peak, their abilities will skyrocket, and above all, they will be more productive. Let us help you build a winning team.

Creating Trust
Score big points with a team whose members trust one another. Trust is the core of any efficient and effective work team.

Resolving Issues
Save money by supporting your work team's development of proactive skills that will enable them to resolve workplace issues they encounter.

Planning Proactively
Give your team new direction and positive focus by empowering them to develop a strategic plan using powerful appreciative inquiry techniques.

Communicating Effectively
Provide the highest quality product and service to your clients by developing your work team's communication strategies and abilities.

Manifesting Personal Development
Create empowered groups of people who are regularly looking withinthemselves for growth, development, motivation, and understanding.

Realizing Your Results
Create experiences that yield your desired outcomes. Ask us how we can customize a program just for you.

If you would like to explore our innovative and truly nontraditional team-building adventures, check us out online at www.tylerhayden.com or give us a call toll free at 866.4.GO.PLAY (866.446.7529). We believe in working hard and playing hard. And we are good at playing hard!

Want to Read More?

Livin' Life Large - *Simple Actions that Create Success*
This fun to read personal development book uses east coast wisdom to create long term life satisfaction. A great read and a great gift.
(Published 2005; ISBN:1-897050-03-8)

Catchin' the Carrot – *Personal Strategic Plan to Success*
This personal planning document is for those who strive to achieve more in life. You will quickly and easily gain a better understanding of where you are, where you're going, and how to get there.
(Published 2004; ISBN:0-9734589-1-7)

Leader's Pack: A Leadership Training Resource Package
This resource is a comprehensive guide to nontraditional soft-skill development experiences. This interactive CD-ROM is easy to use and jam packed with our favorite client-approved activities.
(Published 2000; ISBN:1-897050-00-3)

No Ordinary, Regular Type of Day!
This children's book focuses on the idea that when you believe in yourself, you can achieve anything.
(Published 2000)

Gettin' Off The Treadmill – Activities that take you way outside the box! Eleven weeks of nontraditional experiential learning tools that can help you to explore your priorities and make some changes in your life. You have to experience it to truly understand its power. (Published 2004; ISBN: 0-9734589-2-5)

Teamleader – Because where you take them is as important as how you get them there – Learn Tyler's innovative approach to facilitating learning, which he calls Productivity Processing. In addition, learn to conduct effective icebreaker sessions, build retreat programs, evaluate training events, and much more. (Published 2004; ISBN: 0-9734589-0-9)

Summer Staff Training Guide – *A Retreat Plan and Valuable Information for Summer Recreation Leaders* Recreation staff are known for their high turnover and short contracts. This guide will take you through a multiple-day retreat program that will explore core competencies of an effective summer recreation leader. (Published 2004; ISBN:0-897050-02-X)

Environmental Learning – *Gettin' Dirty is Fun!* This is an introductory guide to the effective facilitation of environmental learning. It explores the educational pursuit from theory to delivery and all points in between. (Published 2004; ISBN: 1-897050-01-1)

All these resources are available to order or download at *www.tylerhayden.com*. Drop by and check them out!

Notes

Notes

Notes

Notes

Notes

Notes

LaVergne, TN USA
20 July 2010
190083LV00001B/7/A

Avertissement

Merci beaucoup d'avoir choisi Atteindre ses buts (« Catchin' the Carrot »). Je sais que vous utiliserez sans difficulté cet outil de planification personnel qui vous aidera à imprimer une orientation stratégique à votre cheminement vers la prospérité. Je vous invite volontiers à me communiquer vos histoires à succès.

En cours de route, si vous avez des questions sur la façon d'utiliser cet outil, n'hésitez pas à communiquer avec nos bureaux en ligne à www.tylerhayden.com et vous recevrez une réponse rapide.

Encore une fois, merci d'avoir choisi Atteindre ses buts (« Catchin' the Carrot »). J'ai hâte d'entendre parler de votre prospérité personnelle.

Tyler Hayden

Pour de plus amples renseignements sur les outils de perfectionnement personnel ou pour réserver un exposé en personne, communiquez avec le bureau de votre conférencier favori ou visitez-nous en ligne à l'adresse suivante :

www.tylerhayden.com

Après une conférence, quelqu'un me demande inévitablement quelles « choses » j'ai faites pour arriver si jeune à une aussi grande prospérité. Franchement, cette question m'embarrasse. Je suis un gars assez simple et assez ordinaire. Je fais moi-même le plein de mon auto, j'aime ma famille et je sors mes propres déchets et produits recyclables, de sorte que j'ignore au juste de quelles « choses » on veut parler.

Il m'a fallu longtemps pour comprendre que, même si je ne suis pas différent des autres, il semble que j'aborde la vie autrement. C'est ce dont parle Atteindre ses buts (« Catchin' the Carrot ») : faire « les choses » autrement.

Autrement, ça veut dire quoi au juste? Eh bien, ça veut dire passer par de petites « choses » qui, à la longue, entraînent une réalisation magnifique. Ces petites étapes sont des éléments individuels de la vie qui touchent tous cet être magnifique que vous êtes.

Ce que j'ai fait autrement par rapport à beaucoup de gens que je connais, c'est apprendre d'abord à me connaître moi-même, puis à construire autour de moi une vie qui me rende heureux. La plupart de mes amis et collègues s'y sont pris à l'envers et ont cherché le bonheur en s'entourant d'éléments de vie qui devraient contribuer à celui-ci. À la longue, ils se fixent en un lieu où ils sont heureux, ou ils apprennent à l'être dans le lieu où ils aboutissent.

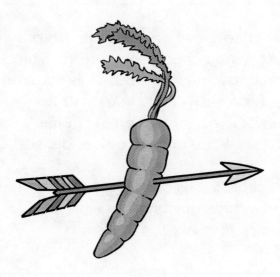

Mes amis, ne vous fixez jamais. Prenez d'abord la voie la plus difficile qui consiste à se connaître en premier lieu, puis à construire autour de soi une vie stimulante. Voilà la « chose » importante.

Je vais vous aider à le faire avec Atteindre ses buts (« Catchin' the Carrot »), grâce à huit étapes faciles. C'est le commencement. Après ce processus, vous devrez revoir votre travail à peu près chaque mois et en ajuster le contenu, car vous commencerez à changer votre vie devant vos propres yeux. Même s'il s'agit d'un processus qui durera une vie entière, plus vous commencerez tôt à prendre le temps de vous connaître, plus tôt vous en réaliserez les avantages.

Présentation

Écrivez une brève présentation de vous-même. C'est le moment ou jamais de vous mettre en valeur. Imaginez que vous vous adressez au « directeur de la vie » et que vous avez dix secondes pour le convaincre que vous êtes la bonne personne pour une tâche. Votre énoncé devrait détailler :

- les « choses » les plus importantes dans votre vie,
- votre histoire personnelle,
- où vous vous voyez à l'avenir.

Essayez ça tout de suite. Rappelez-vous de revenir à cette étape et de l'ajuster quand vous aurez achevé le plan. Vous apprendrez à vous connaître au fur et à mesure, et cet énoncé devra être révisé.

5

haque grande entreprise a un énoncé de mission qui l'oriente vers le succès. Pour « atteindre vos buts » (« Catchin' the Carrot »), vous devez savoir quels sont les vôtres, afin d'arriver vous aussi au succès.

Votre mission doit être un court énoncé de ralliement que vous pouvez facilement retenir. Par exemple, « Jeanne Lalonde est une personne sociable et fiable qui fournit un rendement élevé au travail et qui est une bénévole active dans la collectivité » ou « Jacques Lebrun est un homme calme et athlétique, pour qui la réparation de véhicules automobiles étrangers et canadiens n'a plus de secrets et qui trouve du temps de qualité à passer avec sa famille et ses amis ».

Votre énoncé devrait répondre aux questions suivantes :

- Quelle fonction exercerez-vous à titre individuel?
- Pour qui l'exercerez-vous?
- Comment l'exercerez-vous?

Quelle Fonction?

_____
_____
_____
_____

Pour Qui?

_____
_____
_____
_____

Comment?

_____
_____
_____
_____

Mission...

_____
_____
_____
_____
_____
_____

Chacune de nos décisions personnelles est influencée par un ensemble de valeurs. Par exemple, on peut choisir de ne pas laisser traîner de déchets parce qu'on respecte l'environnement où l'on habite, ou encore faire de l'exercice parce qu'on accorde de l'importance au succès de son équipe de basket-ball. Nos actions peuvent souvent s'expliquer par nos valeurs centrales.

Quelles sont vos valeurs centrales? La famille? Les amis? Le succès? La santé? L'argent? L'apprentissage? Le respect? Les possibilités sont aussi diverses que nous le sommes nous-mêmes. Certaines de mes valeurs fondamentales sont le respect des autres, le souci d'être un éducateur de pointe, le plaisir, le souci à l'égard des gens que j'aime et le maintien des plus hautes normes dans tout ce que je fais. La compréhension de vos valeurs vous aidera à mieux vous comprendre et à prendre de meilleures décisions.

Quelles sont vos valeurs? Énumérez-les ci-dessous et choisissez-en trois au maximum.

_____ _____

_____ _____

_____ _____

_____ _____

3
Valeurs...

_____ _____

_____ _____ ┌─────────────┐
                                   │   │
_____ _____ │   │
                                   └─────────────┘
_____ _____

_____ _____ ┌─────────────┐
                                   │   │
_____ _____ │   │
                                   └─────────────┘
_____ _____

_____ _____ ┌─────────────┐
                                   │   │
_____ _____ │   │
                                   └─────────────┘
_____ _____

_____ _____

_____ _____

_____ _____

9

Objectifs

Prenez un moment pour relire votre mission personnelle. À quoi vous êtes-vous engagé(e) dans cet énoncé? Quelles sont les choses que vous devez faire pour atteindre ce but? Devez-vous, par exemple, suivre des cours du soir, vous porter volontaire pour des projets de l'entreprise ou consacrer plus de temps à votre famille? Quelles étapes spécifiques devez-vous prendre pour vous acquitter de cette mission?

Dans la section suivante, fixez des objectifs qui vous aideront à réaliser votre mission. Ceux-ci devraient être simples, mesurables, réalisables, réalistes et fermes. Par exemple, Jacques pourrait vouloir notamment ouvrir une entreprise de réparation de véhicules automobiles étrangers en 2010, ou emmener sa famille, chaque été, passer une semaine de vacances, à partir de cette année. Que devez-vous faire particulièrement pour atteindre vos objectifs?

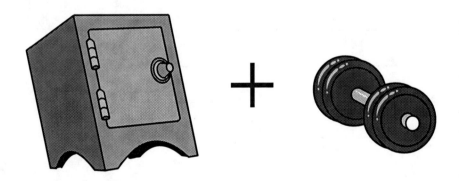

Objectif 1

_____

_____

_____

Objectif 2

_____

_____

_____

Objectif 3

_____

_____

_____

Objectif 4

_____

_____

_____

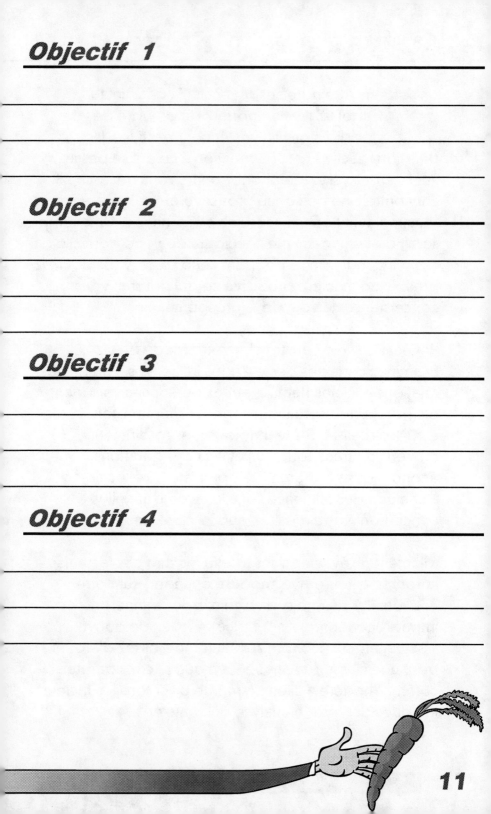

Analyse du contexte

Dans Atteindre ses objectifs (« Catchin' the Carrot »), il est important de prendre des décisions proactives et non réactives. Une décision réactive est une réaction à ce qui se passe. Par exemple, si le téléphone sonne, vous décrochez. Par contre, une personne proactive prévoit d'avance sa réaction avant que la cause ne se manifeste. Un exemple serait d'établir des voies de sortie de votre domicile en cas d'incendie. En remplissant cette page, vous pourrez prévoir de manière proactive ce qui pourrait vous concerner sur la voie de la prospérité.

Réfléchissez à ce qui touche votre mode de vie. Examinez certaines des grandes influences, comme les relations sociales (famille, autres personnes importantes, etc.), les facteurs politiques (gouvernement, lois, taxes, etc.), les réalisations technologiques (ordinateurs, moyens de transport, etc.) et les considérations économiques (emprunts, emploi, etc.). Réfléchissez à ces grandes influences et à la façon dont elles concernent votre mission, puis inscrivez-les.

Maintenant, évaluez dans quelle mesure ces facteurs auront un effet (grave, modéré ou léger) sur votre mission. Par exemple, dans le cas de Jeanne, un impact économique pourrait être le fait de pouvoir « actuellement économiser seulement assez d'argent pour une classe par année », ce que je considérerais comme modéré. Faites de même pour tous les facteurs indiqués dans votre analyse du contexte.

Analyse du contexte | Effet

_____

_____

_____

_____

_____

_____

_____

_____

_____

_____

_____

_____

_____

_____

Vous et moi avons chacun nos propres forces et faiblesses personnelles. Il se peut que vous soyez un bon lecteur (force), mais un mauvais mathématicien (faiblesse), que j'excelle dans la motivation des gens (force), tout en ayant de la difficulté à respecter les échéances (faiblesse). De plus, vous et moi sommes entourés d'occasions et de menaces personnelles et professionnelles. Il se peut que vous habitiez à proximité d'une grande clientèle potentielle (occasion), mais que six gros concurrents se trouvent dans le même parc industriel (menace). Je pourrais avoir d'excellents gènes pour un corps sain (occasion), en ignorant les bonnes techniques d'exercice (menace).

En comprenant ces facteurs, nous pouvons optimiser les choses qui nous avantagent et gérer celles qui pourraient nous entraver. Examinez donc sérieusement la façon dont vous utilisez vos forces et faiblesses dans votre vie. Quels changements pourriez-vous apporter en votre faveur?

Dans les carrés suivants, indiquez, après un remue-méninges, quelles sont vos forces et faiblesses personnelles et professionnelles, ainsi que les occasions et les menaces.

Force	Faiblesse

Occasion	Menace

Considérez votre mission comme le sommet d'un escalier et vos objectifs comme des marches; la planification de l'action est chaque mouvement que vous devez faire pour gravir physiquement chaque marche.

Cette planification consiste à écrire ce que vous devez spécifiquement faire pour atteindre vos objectifs. Commencez par inscrire les objectifs que vous avez indiqués tout à l'heure, puis concentrez-vous sur chacun d'eux et inscrivez les mouvements (actions) que vous devez faire pour l'atteindre. Par exemple, l'un des objectifs de Jacques consistait à « passer chaque été des vacances d'une semaine en famille à partir de cette année ». Ses étapes pourraient être les suivantes :

1. commencer à verser 150 $ par mois dans un compte d'épargne spécial;
2. discuter avec la famille de ce que l'on aimerait faire cet été-là;
3. examiner les possibilités relatives à des vacances d'une semaine;
4. prendre les dispositions nécessaires de voyage (avion, hôtels, durée de vacances, etc.).

Vous avez compris? Maintenant allez-y!

Objectif 1

_____

_____

_____

Objectif 2

_____

_____

_____

Objectif 3

_____

_____

_____

Objectif 4

_____

_____

_____

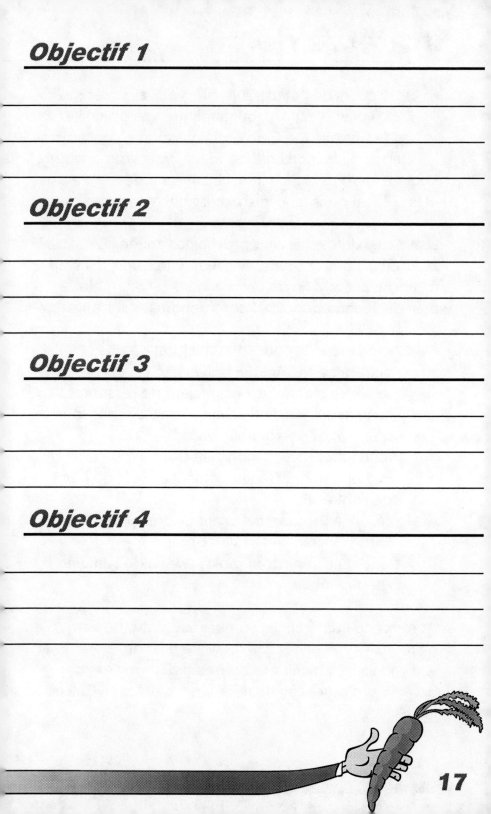

Stratégie de cinq ans

Au cours de l'étape suivante, vous avez rédigé un plan d'action pour atteindre vos objectifs (« Catchin' the Carrot »). Vous avez alors choisi les étapes de la marche ascendante vers votre mission. Vous devez maintenant franchir chacune de ces étapes et les placer dans un ordre accessible et logique.

Écrivez les dates des cinq prochaines années (2004, 2005, 2006, etc.). Sous chacune, inscrivez, une à une, les étapes à franchir avant la fin de cette année. Par exemple, le plan de Jeanne pour 2004 comprendra les suivantes :

- s'inscrire à un cours d'administration des entreprises à l'Acadia University;
- explorer les lacunes en matière de ressources humaines à son lieu actuel d'emploi, sous forme d'un projet personnel;
- rencontrer son gestionnaire pour exprimer son intérêt à siéger bénévolement au sein de comités de l'entreprise;
- créer un programme d'entraînement aérobic trois jours par semaine et s'en occuper;
- faire du camping au moins une fin de semaine chaque mois.

Après cette étape finale, commencez à mettre votre plan en route. Commencez à vivre votre mission, à exprimer vos valeurs, à franchir vos étapes, à déterminer vos occasions d'agir et à atteindre vos objectifs (« Catchin' the Carrot »).

1

2

3

4